Inventions That Shaped the World

THE MICROSCOPE

CHRISTINE PETERSEN

Franklin Watts
A Division of Scholastic Inc.
New York • Toronto • London • Auckland • Sydney
Mexico City • New Delhi • Hong Kong
Danbury, Connecticut

Photographs © 2006: Corbis Images: 18, 20 (Archivo Iconografico, S.A.), cover bottom right, 55, 57 (Bettmann), 12 (Matthias Kulka), chapter opener-cell, 15, 54 (Royalty-Free); Getty Images: 48 (Keith Brofsky/Photodisc Green), 51 (Geostock/Photodisc Green), 58 (Keystone/Hulton Archive); Mary Evans Picture Library: 45 (Wolf/Explorer Archives), cover top right; Peter Arnold Inc./Volker Steger: 31, 62; Photo Researchers, NY: 53 (Biophoto Associates), 28, 32 (Dr. Jeremy Burgess), 56 (Scott Camazine), 7 (James Cavallini), 69 (Nicolas Edwige), 49 (Spencer Grant), 65 (James Holmes), 59 (James King-Holmes), cover left (LBNL), 50 (LBNL/Science Source), 24 (Omikron), 13 (David Parker), 38 (Alfred Pasieka), 9, 60 (Science Source), 16 (Paul Singh-Roy), 52 (SPL), 23 (Sheila Terry), 35 (Gianni Tortoli), 67 (USDA/Nature Souce); Phototake: 61 (Mauritius/GMBH), 66 (Richard T. Nowitz), 10 (Ken Wagner); The Image Works: 27 (Ann Ronan Picture Library/HIP), 6 (Bob Daemmrich), 42 (Liverati/SSPL), chapter opener-microscope (Science Museum, London/Topham-HIP), 33 (Science Museum, London/SSPL), 19, 26, 43, 63 (SSPL).

Illustration by J. T. Morrow

Cover design by The Design Lab
Book production by The Design Lab

Library of Congress Cataloging-in-Publication Data
Petersen, Christine.
The microscope / Christine Petersen.
p. cm. — (Inventions that shaped the world)
Includes bibliographical references and index.
ISBN 0-531-12408-8 (lib. bdg.) 0-531-13902-6 (pbk.)
1. Microscopes—History—Juvenile literature. 2. Microscopes—Juvenile literature. I. Title. II. Series.
QH278.P48 2006
502'.8'2—dc22 2005007257

 Published in 2006 by Franklin Watts, an imprint of Scholastic Library Publishing. Published simultaneously in Canada.
Printed in China.
4 5 6 7 8 9 10 R 15 14 13 12 11 10 62

Contents

CHAPTER ONE

The Unknown Is Revealed

On a warm autumn afternoon, forty middle school students sit on the banks of a narrow, rushing stream. They cluster in groups like football players in a huddle, each waiting for a turn to peer through a small, portable microscope. Now and then a student calls out excitedly, "I've got a dragonfly larva!" or "What is that?" Simple and inexpensive, these microscopes make anything in the water look twenty-five times larger than it actually is—offering details of the unknown and making known objects unrecognizable.

The students are astonished by what they see—mayfly larvae with sharp "tails" as long as their bodies, water boatmen with legs shaped (and used) like oars, caddis fly larvae with tufts of hair sprouting from their thin bodies. The teacher has said that certain microscopic organisms cannot

A sample of water is filled with living things too small to be seen without a microscope.

live in polluted water. The organisms the students find will help determine whether this stream is healthy or polluted.

Seeing Another World

Nearly four centuries ago, scientists were discovering microscopic organisms such as these for the first time. Before the mid-seventeenth century, people had no reason to imagine that Earth's water, soil, and air were full of organisms too small to see with the naked eye. The invention of microscopes opened up a world people never dreamed existed. It is populated by thousands of species of life-forms—large and small—whose bodies are made up of even smaller cells, which in turn are made of ***atoms.*** As microscopes have become more powerful, scientists have even been able to see the parts of atoms, some so small they must be magnified millions of times to be visible.

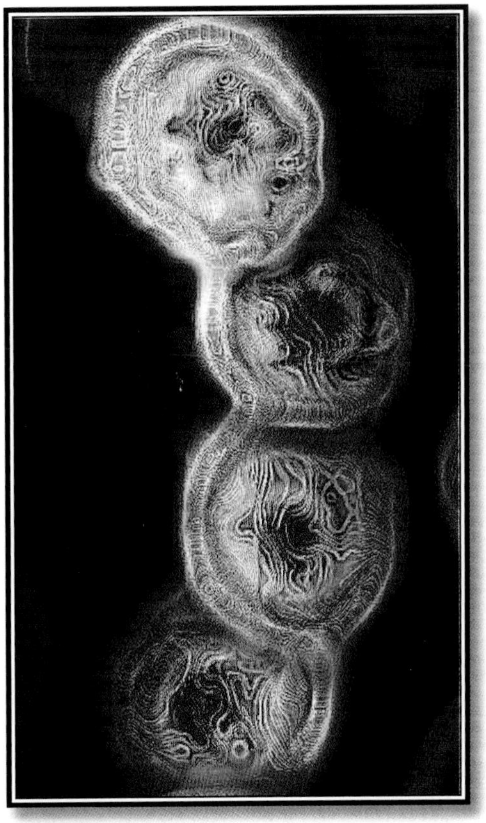

Hundreds of years ago, scientists had no idea that microorganisms, such as Streptococcus *bacteria, existed.*

Today, we take this knowledge for granted. Yet it took many generations and a lot of trial and error before scientists had enough information to build the first microscope. First, they had to understand how light, vision, and magnification work. To follow that trail of discovery, we must look back more than 2,500 years ago, to the earliest days of science.

The Origins of Science

Science has its roots in the part of the world now known as Greece, Italy, and Turkey, along the Aegean Sea. There, during the Roman Empire (753 B.C.–A.D. 476), a great civilization arose. A thriving trade was established with nations to the east, bringing new ideas from faraway lands. In this culture, ideas were very important. Certain members of society, called philosophers, spent their whole lives trying to make sense of the world and humans' place in it.

Light was a topic of great interest to some of these ancient scholars. A Greek mathematician named Pythagoras, who lived in the sixth century B.C., looked for the source of light. He believed that it came from inside people, escaping through their eyes like ribbons. When light-ribbons came into contact with objects, he said, the objects became visible. Later philosophers wondered what form light takes. Is it a particle, a tiny piece of solid material, which travels from the eye to outside objects? Or is it a kind of moving energy?

From Aristotle to Ptolemy

The famous Greek teacher Aristotle (384–322 B.C.) suggested that light travels in undulating waves, like those on the surface of the ocean. Euclid, a Greek mathematician who was born just before Aristotle died, agreed that light moves in waves. He added the idea that light waves flow in straight lines until something blocks their path.

Claudius Ptolemaeus (who is also called Ptolemy) was an astronomer, mathematician, and geographer who lived in Egypt in the second century A.D. Unlike the philosophers before him, whose theories were constructed using observation and logic, Ptolemy conducted experiments—tests that helped prove his ideas. Although he is remembered today mostly for his mistaken theory that Earth is the center of the universe, Ptolemy made some brilliant discoveries about the way light interacts with different ***media,*** or substances that interact differently with light.

Aristotle was a Greek philosopher and teacher who studied in Athens under Plato.

In one experiment, Ptolemy placed a stick in a pool of water. He noticed that it seemed to bend. Pulling the stick out of the water proved that it had not actually bent. Ptolemy decided that the stick appeared to bend in water

A wooden dowel in a glass of water can be used to demonstrate light refraction.

because light rays slow down as they go from air into water. He concluded that the slowing of light rays causes them to change direction. As a result, any object in the water appears slightly to one side of its actual position. Ptolemy eventually proved that light moves fastest through air, a little slower through water, and slower yet through glass. He then calculated the angle at which light rays bend in different media. Today, the bending of light is known as ***refraction.***

Magnification was another phenomenon that interested ancient scientists. Long before the Roman Empire, people knew that certain materials ***magnify*** other objects, making them look larger. Water has this effect, which can be observed when rain falls on a leaf or other surface. Look down through the drop of water: whatever is below appears larger. Glass is another material that magnifies. It was commonly used to make jewelry and ornaments in Egypt as long as 3,500 years ago, and citizens of the Roman Empire used it in their everyday lives. The philosopher Seneca (4 B.C.–A.D. 65) observed magnification through glass and wrote that "letters, though small and indistinct, are seen enlarged and more distinctly through a glass globe filled with water."

Almost one thousand years passed before the next important discoveries about light and magnification were made. During that time, the Roman Empire fell. Invaders from the north and east took over the empire's western lands, including the great city of Rome. These people brought different religions and cultures, and they were not interested in science. Fortunately, the eastern part of the empire, called Byzantium, remained peaceful for several more centuries. Here scientists were able to continue their study of the natural world.

Alhazen's Advances

Byzantine scientists translated the works of ancient philosophers into their own language, Arabic. Great libraries were built to contain these books. Alhazen (A.D. 962–1038) was an Arab scientist who translated the writings of Euclid and Ptolemy. Inspired by their ideas, he decided to conduct experiments with light. Among these was a test to see whether light really travels in a straight line, as Euclid had suggested. Alhazen set up a screen near a wall and punched a small hole in its center. On the side of the screen opposite the wall, he placed three candles at different angles to the hole. When he lit the candles, three distinct spots of light appeared on the wall. It was clear that the light from each candle shone through the hole, then continued in a straight line beyond it.

These observations proved Euclid right. They also forced Alhazen to disagree with Pythagoras's belief, held

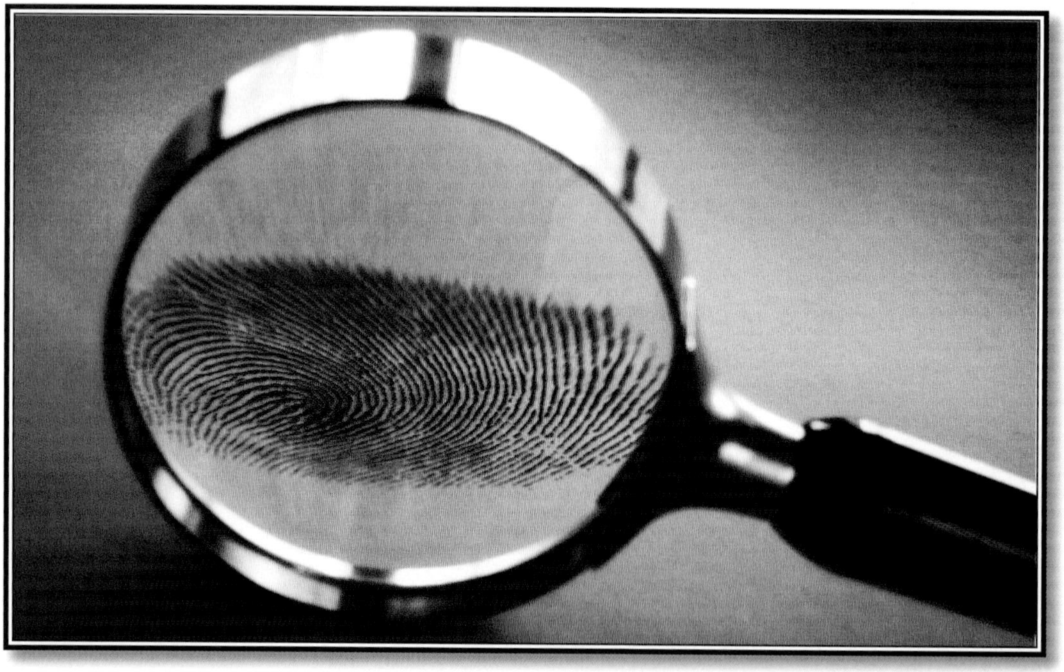

A fingerprint as viewed with a magnifying glass. Even ancient scientists knew that glass was a material that magnifies objects.

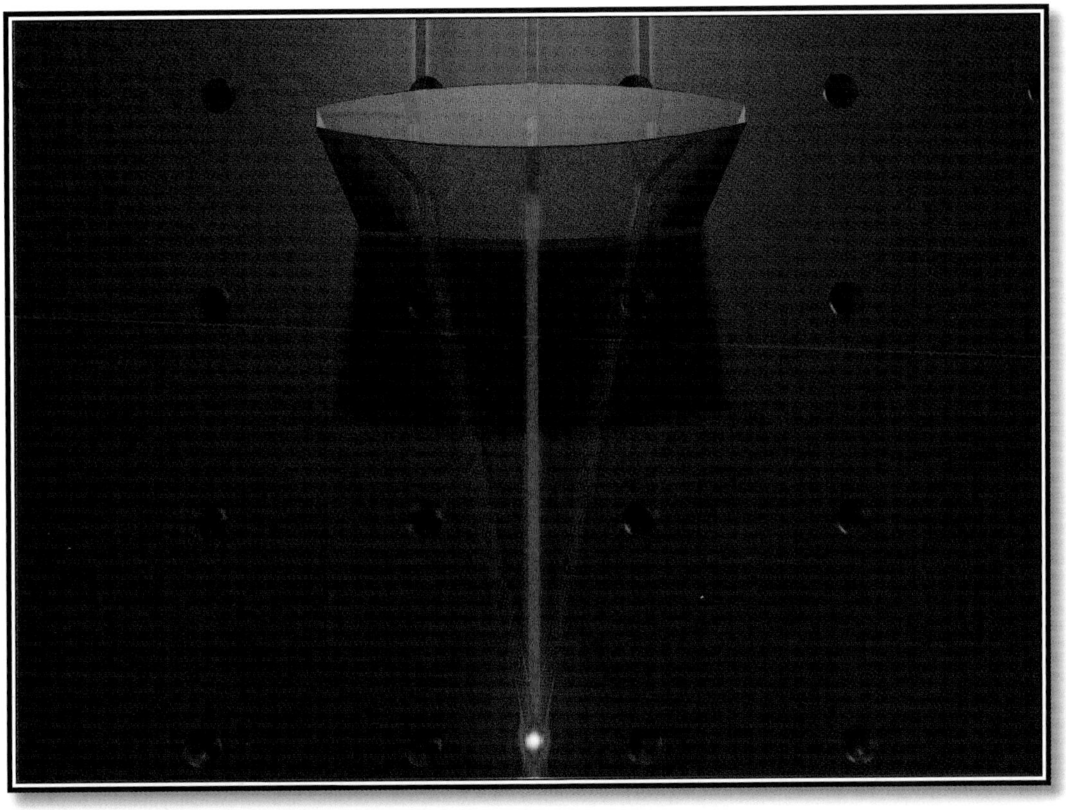

Light beams that pass through a biconvex lens bend so that they come together. Alhazen was one of the first scientists to experiment with lenses.

for 1,500 years, that light came from the eye. Instead, he said, eyes absorb light that they collect from the surroundings. Alhazen noticed that some objects—the Sun, candles, and fireflies, for example—make their own light. All other objects ***reflect*** light, meaning light bounces off their surfaces.

From Ptolemy, Alhazen knew that light rays refract as they pass from air into denser media. He began to experiment with ***lenses*** (curved pieces of glass or other clear material) in order to understand exactly how this bending takes place. He discovered that the shape of a lens determines the size of the image it produces—thicker, rounder lenses magnify more than thin lenses.

Alhazen's research, and that of the ancient Greek scientists who came before him, revealed the three principles that explain how magnification happens. First, light travels in a straight line. Second, light rays bend when they pass from air into a denser medium. Finally, the shape and thickness of a lens controls the angle at which light refracts, which in turn determines the size of the magnified image.

In general, light rays tend to refract away from the thinnest part of a lens. As a result, when light rays pass through a ***convex lens***—one that is thicker in the center than at the edges—they are bent inward. Refracted rays cross each other's paths at a point some distance from the center of the lens. This distance is called a ***focal length.*** The thicker the lens, the shorter its focal length. If an object is placed less than one focal length from a convex lens, it will appear larger than it actually is. In other words, it will be magnified.

Although these were significant realizations, it was another 250 years before science or society would find a way to put this knowledge to use. What followed was a revolution that continues in modern times.

CHAPTER TWO

A New Way of Looking at the World

While many animals rely heavily on the senses of smell or hearing, humans are mainly visual animals. We obtain as much as two-thirds of our information about the world through our eyes. The position of our eyes (at the front of our heads, rather than to the sides as they are in deer, fish, and most birds) permits us to see far into the distance and in three dimensions. We can distin-

Humans usually depend on their sense of sight more than any other sense.

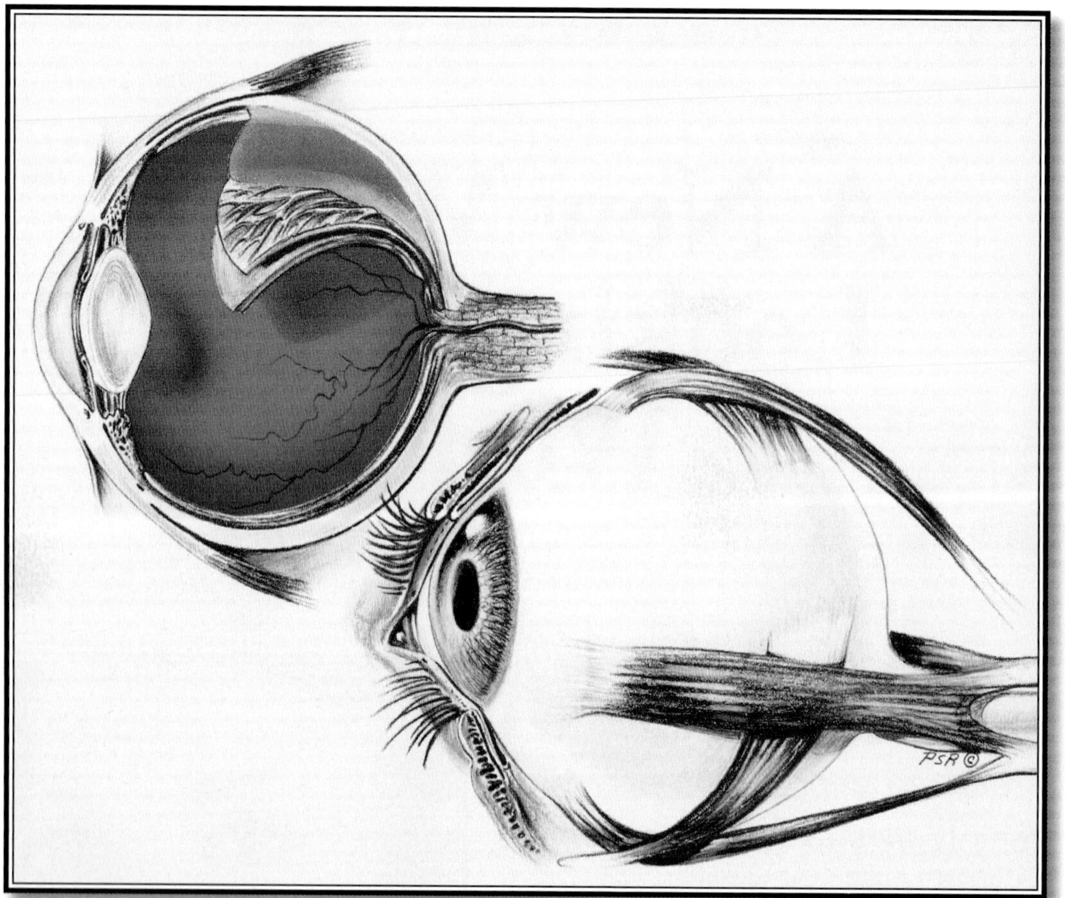

The tiny muscles in the human eye can change the size of the pupil to control the amount of light that enters the eye.

guish between objects, such as the individual letters and punctuation marks printed on this page, that are as little as four-thousandths of an inch (0.1 millimeter) apart. And because we are active in the daytime, human eyes are built to see color. These adaptations allow us to see a rich and complex world and respond quickly to survive in it.

Unfortunately, many people are born with weak eye muscles or with slight imperfections of the eye that affect their vision. Our eyes commonly weaken as we age, as well. Throughout history, poor eyesight has had a tremendous impact on the quality of people's lives. And it was one of the main reasons magnifying lenses became popular in the late thirteenth century.

How Does the Eye See?

When light rays strike the human eye, they pass through the cornea, a thin "envelope" surrounding the eye. The cornea refracts light inward, toward the colored iris and the dark pupil. The pupil controls how much light enters the eye. The iris contains muscles that open the pupil wider in dim situations and shrink it in glaring light. Once past the pupil, light strikes the eye lens and angles inward again. The eye's lens is far more flexible than any man-made lens. Surrounded by fast-acting muscles, the lens can be pulled thinner or squished into a thicker shape to focus on objects at different distances.

Light refracted through the lens strikes the retina, at the back of the eye. The retina is covered with two types of tiny cells called rods and cones. Rods are sensitive to black and white, while cones detect color. Each contains a nerve that leads to the brain, which constructs a picture from all the different pieces of information it receives.

Bringing the World into Focus

After the decline of the Roman Empire seven hundred years before, Europe fell into disarray. During most of this period (called the Middle Ages), there were no great cities, no clear system of government, and no common language or currency. Education was almost nonexistent. Most people had no time or skills to ponder the workings of the natural world. Church leaders also discouraged the study of science. They taught that nature was a mystery humans were not meant to understand. Few people in Europe knew what lenses were or had much use for them.

That began to change in the eleventh century. In the year 1080, the troops of King Alfonso VI took control of most of Spain. They entered the city of Toledo, which had long been controlled by Muslims. Soldiers were surprised to find a massive library in Toledo, containing hundreds of books written in Arabic. Alongside translations of the ancient philosophers, including those made by Alhazen, were many recent books written by Arab scientists and philosophers. This sud-

An illustration from a book written in the early eleventh century

Roger Bacon is often considered the first modern scientist because of his emphasis on experimentation.

den access to information inspired a new wave of scholarship among Europeans. Over time, education systems began to improve. But as more people learned to read, poor vision became a serious problem.

In the late 1260s, an English monk and scientist named Roger Bacon (1220–1292) wrote a book called *Opus Majus*. This book was a compilation of scientific knowledge, and it included information about ***optics*** (the study of light). In it, Bacon wrote that convex lenses could serve as "instruments useful to old men and those whose sight is weakened, who in such a way will be able to see the letters sufficiently enlarged, however small they are." Afterward, the demand for magnifying glasses—convex lenses mounted in a frame, usually with a handle—quickly grew throughout Europe.

Italian physicist Salvino d'Armati gets credit for inventing eyeglasses between 1285 and 1300. D'Armati's

Nicholas of Cusa was born in 1401. He was a priest, mathematician, and scientist.

eyesight was terrible. Frustrated by having to hold a magnifying lens while he worked, he cleverly fitted two convex lenses side-by-side inside a metal frame. The frame perched upon the bridge of his nose, improving his vision while leaving both his hands free. His friend, a priest named Alessandro della Spina, saw d'Armati's eyeglasses and decided to make some for himself. Then he wrote and published an explanation of the manufacturing process. In thirteenth-century Italy, that was the equivalent of filing for a patent. Before long, people around Europe were wearing eyeglasses to help them read.

Eyeglasses for Everyone

In 1451, German scholar Nicholas of Cusa was working with ***concave lenses,*** or lenses that are thinner at the center than around the edges. He observed that they make distant objects appear closer. It occurred to Nicholas that concave lenses might correct nearsightedness (weak long-distance vision). He was right. Eyeglasses were soon available to help nearsighted people, those who could not see distant objects clearly. These, along with the existing eyeglasses for farsighted people (those with weak short-distance vision), allowed many people to enjoy sharp eyesight again.

The Renaissance

Between 1451 and 1456, the invention of movable metal type—the printing press—marked a turning point in European culture and history. Historians call this period the Renaissance, a French word meaning "rebirth." For the first time, books could be reproduced quickly and in large numbers instead of being painstakingly written by hand or carved into woodblocks for printing. Great books soon circulated around Europe, allowing people to share ideas and information.

As part of this rebirth, lens makers and scientists began investigating innovative uses for magnifying lenses. By the fifteenth century, ***simple microscopes,*** consisting of narrow tubes with single convex lenses inside, were available in most European cities. The lenses used in these instruments were very small, and the process for grinding and polishing them was detailed and time-consuming. As a result, microscopes were extremely expensive. Only the wealthiest people—or scientists who had wealthy supporters—could own them. Looking through them was considered a special form of entertainment reserved for an elite part of society, and skilled lens makers were in high demand.

Hans and Zacharias Janssen were ready to meet that demand. About 1590, young Zacharias was learning to be a lens maker. He got the idea that two lenses might provide stronger magnification than one. With his father's help, he constructed the first ***compound microscope***—a microscope containing more than one lens, in which the second lens further magnifies the image created by the first lens.

Simple and compound microscopes using glass lenses can be categorized together as light microscopes, because both require light to produce images. Early light microscopes (and even some used today) took advantage of ambient light, or light from their surroundings. Direct sunlight was best, because of its brightness. Scientists did most of their work standing in a window or doorway, in order to catch rays of sunlight streaming down from outside. At times when natural lighting was poor, they placed candles or lamps near the microscope.

CHAPTER THREE

Hooke and Leeuwenhoek—Men with a Vision

A scientist uses candles for extra light as he examines animal tissue under a microscope.

Countless philosophers, scientists, and lens makers contributed to the invention of microscopes. Credit for making microscopes into the important tools they are today, however, must go to the early scientists who used them in innovative ways. Two seventeenth-century microscopists led the way: Robert Hooke and Antonie van Leeuwenhoek.

Hooke Finds Cells

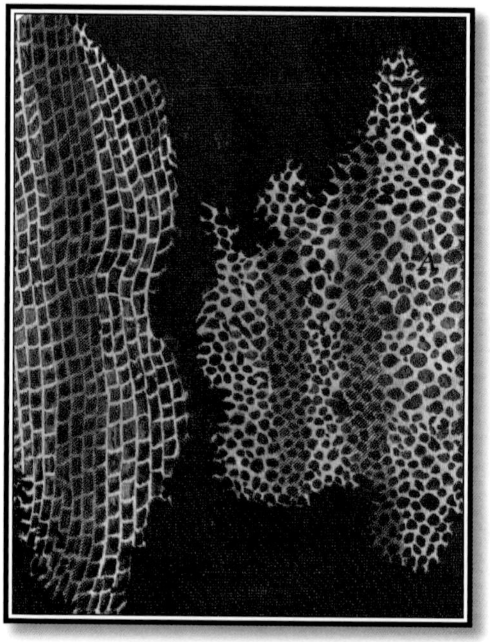

Robert Hooke included this illustration of cork cells in Micrographia.

Robert Hooke was born in England on July 18, 1635. Small and weak as a boy, he spent most of his time indoors reading about science and learning to draw. Later, at Oxford University, Hooke studied with some of the greatest scientists of the day. In 1663, his drawings of human capillaries (the tiniest blood vessels) caught the attention of the Royal Society of London. Formed only a year before, the Royal Society had already established a reputation as one of the most important scientific organizations in Europe. Impressed with Hooke's work, members of the society asked the young scientist to perform microscope demonstrations at their weekly meetings.

During one of the earliest demonstrations, Hooke decided to examine cork. After slicing a piece so thin it was almost transparent, he placed the specimen under his microscope. He saw what looked like lines of empty boxes. Because they resembled a map of the tiny rooms monks lived in, he called these boxes by the same name: cells (from the Latin word *cellula*, or "small room"). Hooke was the first person to observe and describe cells, which are now known to be the basic units from which all life is built.

The Royal Society

In the mid-seventeenth century, English scientists began meeting to share ideas and conduct scientific experiments. King Charles II admired their work, and in 1660 he allowed them to start a scientific organization. The group called itself The Royal Society of London for Improving Natural Knowledge. Full members were chosen by election and called Fellows. Today, almost 350 years after its establishment, the Royal Society continues to support and encourage the work of some of the world's leading scientists.

Hooke's drawings and descriptions were originally published in the Royal Society's journal, *Philosophical Transactions*. In 1665, they were compiled into a book called *Micrographia* ("small drawings"). People were fascinated by this first-ever, close-up look at small organisms. *Micrographia* became a sort of best seller at the time—and it is still in print today.

Hooke Improves the Microscope

In his lifetime, Hooke invented a number of improvements that made compound microscopes easier to use. At

Hooke's compound microscope and illuminating system were reconstructed in 2000 using the illustration and description in Micrographia.

the time, ambient light was the only way to illuminate specimens. This was inefficient, however—candlelight was too weak, and sunlight came and went, depending on the time of day and the weather. To obtain better lighting, Hooke placed a globe of water between a lamp and his microscope. As lamplight passed through the globe, its rays were refracted inward. Where the rays crossed paths, the light was far brighter. By placing the microscope at this point, the specimen received much greater illumination. Modern microscopes contain similar lighting systems, called ***condensers,*** to improve lighting.

Hooke also built microscopes that were more comfortable to look through. Like other microscopes of the time, his was attached to a base so it could stand on its own.

Instead of being fixed to the base, however, Hooke's microscope was attached to the base with a screw, allowing the instrument to be tilted back and forth. The observer now had the option to sit while working.

Antonie van Leeuwenhoek

Thonis Philipszoon, better known as Antonie van Leeuwenhoek, was another brilliant microscopist, born on October 24, 1632, in Delft, Holland. He left school at the age of sixteen and moved to another town, where he worked as an apprentice in the shop of a fabric merchant. Fabric merchants often used convex magnifying lenses to examine the quality and weave of their materials, and it was in this setting that Leeuwenhoek first encountered microscopes.

Using the microscopes he built, Antonie van Leeuwenhoek discovered the existence of blood cells, bacteria in tooth tartar, and many other things.

From Hobby to History

After completing his apprenticeship in 1654, Leeuwenhoek returned home to Delft. He married, set up his own linen shop, and carried on with his life much like any other seventeenth-century man. Leeuwenhoek had an unusual hobby, however, that made him quite different from his neighbors and friends: he was fascinated by microscopes.

During the first fifteen years after he returned to Delft, Leeuwenhoek learned to grind his own lenses for inspecting fabrics. He taught himself to grind marvelously clear, bead-like convex lenses from glass and quartz. He did this without any formal scientific training and worked in his spare time. Leeuwenhoek's curiosity eventually inspired him to turn those lenses onto objects in the natural world around him. He observed everything he could, from the muscles of whales to the brains of flies.

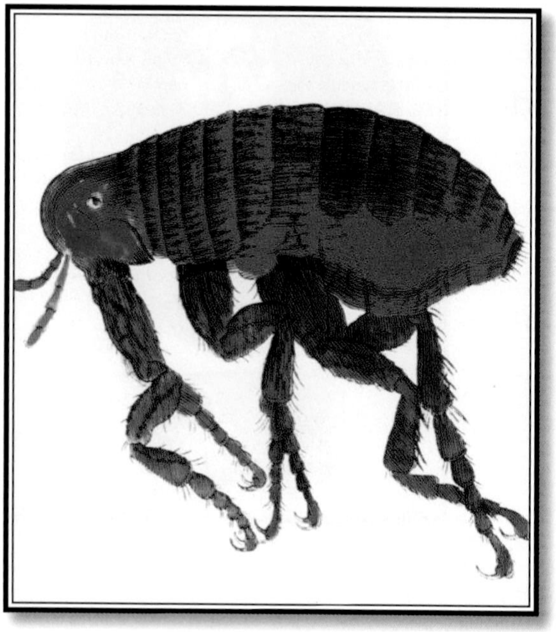

Leeuwenhoek created this detailed drawing of a flea after observing it under a microscope.

During a business trip to England in the 1660s, Leeuwenhoek may have looked at a copy of Robert Hooke's popular book *Micrographia*. He may have marveled at Hooke's intricately detailed drawings. Leeuwenhoek would have made another important realization, as well. While the compound microscopes used by Robert Hooke magnified up to 30X (thirty times the actual size), Leeuwenhoek's handmade simple microscopes achieved magnifications of 250X or more.

In 1673, Dr. Regnier de Graaf wrote a letter to the Royal Society of London describing the brilliant work being done by his friend, Antonie van Leeuwenhoek. Members of the Royal Society respected de Graaf for his microscopic study of the human ovary (a female reproductive organ that produces eggs). The society politely invited Leeuwenhoek to submit a sample of his work, so he prepared a long letter with descriptions and drawings of bees, lice, and fungus. Royal Society members were appalled at Leeuwenhoek's casual, rambling writing style and his lack of formal education: He didn't speak English or Latin, the language of science at that time. But the scholars were deeply impressed with his findings. They invited Leeuwenhoek to continue submitting his work, which was published in *Philosophical Transactions*.

Microscopes allowed Leeuwenhoek to see parts of the world no one—not even experts such as Hooke—knew existed. In 1674, Leeuwenhoek noticed patches of green in the water of a lake. He viewed a sample through a microscope and was astounded by what he saw. Long, winding strands of green filled the water. Between them, tiny creatures swam, spun, and dove. Each was far smaller than any animal he had seen previously. Leeuwenhoek knew he had discovered something amazing. In a letter to the Royal Society, he called the creatures animalcules (Latin for "little animals") and wrote that "among all the marvels that I have discovered in nature, [these are] the most marvelous of all."

Leeuwenhoek's Microscopes

Antonie van Leeuwenhoek built microscopes unlike any made before or since. They consisted of two joined metal plates, each less than 2 inches (5 centimeters) in length. Sandwiched between them, and centered in a hole, was a tiny lens. Specimens were mounted on the point of a needle, which was attached by a screw to one of the plates. The screw could be wound up or down to center the specimen in front of the lens. It could also be moved forward or backward, to achieve focus. Leeuwenhoek's lenses were barely 1/25 of an inch (1 millimeter) thick. The rounded curve of these lenses produced incredibly short focal lengths. To see an image, the microscope had to be held almost in contact with the viewer's eye. Leeuwenhoek made 500 lenses and 250 microscopes, but kept his lens-grinding methods secret. Only nine of his original microscopes remain.

Leeuwenhoek Discovers a Tiny World

Nine years later, Leeuwenhoek wrote to the society about his discovery of even smaller *animalcules*. These he found in material scraped from his own teeth. The creatures were so numerous, he said, that more could live "in the

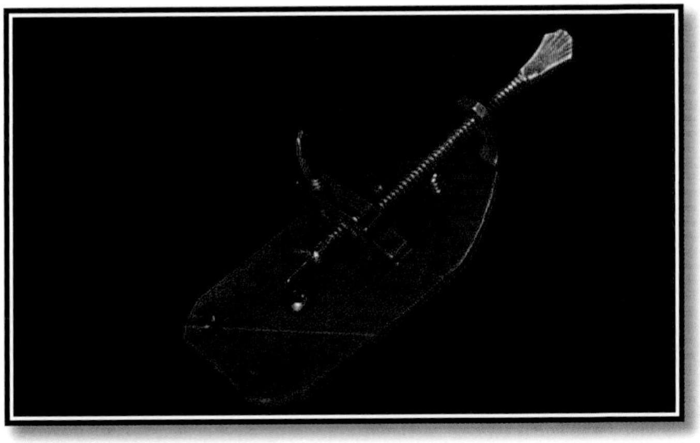

The first of many microscopes built by Leeuwenhoek

scum on the teeth in a man's mouth, than there are men in a whole kingdom." As much as they respected Leeuwenhoek's skill, members of the Royal Society were doubtful that such miniscule organisms could be real. They asked Robert Hooke to duplicate Leeuwenhoek's experiment for proof. Hooke saw the organisms for himself and was forced to admit that his Dutch colleague was correct. Leeuwenhoek had discovered bacteria, the smallest organisms on Earth that are able to live on their own.

The Royal Society bestowed its highest honor on Leeuwenhoek in 1680: he was made a Fellow (lifetime member). Leeuwenhoek was thrilled to be counted among the most respected scientists of his day. But this recognition brought more attention than he wanted. Other scientists, wealthy microscope hobbyists, and even royalty soon began dropping by to get a peek at the wonders revealed under Leeuwenhoek's lenses. Taking this as an intrusion into his work, he showed little patience with the visitors. Leeuwenhoek hovered over his guests and watched their

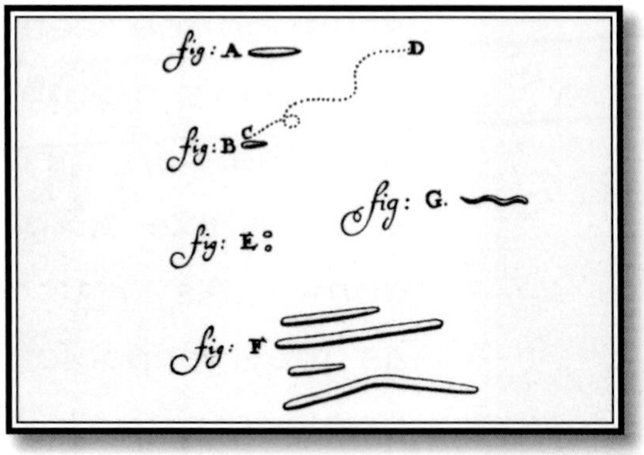

These drawings of animalcules—what we now know as bacteria—were included in Leeuwenhoek's 1683 letter to the Royal Society in London. The letter details his observation of the creatures that he scraped from his teeth.

every move, suspicious that someone would steal one of his microscopes. When they left, he happily went back to work.

Leeuwenhoek continued to build microscopes and examine nature's wonders until his death in 1723, just before his ninety-first birthday. He never visited the Royal Society in person, but he kept in constant contact. Over the course of fifty years, he sent the Fellows more than two hundred letters, containing some of the first-known explanations of the structure of blood cells, the anatomy of insects, and the details of animal reproduction. Leeuwenhoek's letters reveal the painstaking care he took in carrying out his experiments, repeating them over and over again to ensure the accuracy of his results.

After his death, Leeuwenhoek's daughter sent a box to the Royal Society. It contained twenty-six of her father's precious microscopes, each with an original specimen attached. Some of these magnificent tools, and the letters describing his discoveries, can still be found at the Royal Society in London.

CHAPTER FOUR

Building Better Microscopes

The Janssen microscope was the first compound microscope.

In 1590, the Janssen microscope was invented. Bulky and requiring two hands to operate, it was nothing like the compound microscopes used in classrooms and laboratories today. It was made from a long metal tube in three pieces, one fitting snugly inside the other. The largest was about 2 inches (5 cm) in diameter. A concave lens was located at the top of the tube. In modern microscopes, this part is known as the eyepiece. A second, convex lens (called the objective because it sits closest to the object being viewed) was located at the far end of the tube. Focus was achieved by sliding the top and bottom ends of the tubing to adjust the distance between lenses. This first compound microscope produced fuzzy images with a magnification of less than 10X. That seems unimpressive by modern standards, but at the time it was a sign of greater advancements in magnification to come.

From Telescope to Microscope

In 1609, just nineteen years after the Janssen microscope was introduced, Italian scientist and inventor Galileo Galilei built a similar tool for viewing objects at great distances—the telescope. Galileo was equally interested in viewing small objects. By modifying the telescope's design slightly, he was able to produce a compound microscope. Galileo was enthusiastic about what he saw through his microscope. He wrote, "With this tube I have seen flies which look as big as lambs." Yet Galileo found his own microscope hard to use because of its length. As in the Janssen model, the convex and concave lenses had to be placed far apart in order to create a focused image.

German astronomer Johannes Kepler knew that compound microscopes held a lot of promise as scientific tools, and he wondered how they might be made more compact.

Galileo's original telescope is on display at the Institute and Museum of the History of Science in Florence, Italy.

In 1611, he suggested an alternative. Two convex lenses, he said, could form a focused image when placed closer together. This would allow the microscope tube to be shorter. Kepler never built such a microscope, but he had the right idea. Other scientists and lens makers figured out the same solution. By the mid-1600s, compound microscopes using two convex lenses quickly began to appear around Europe.

"Little Eye"

Although the word *microscope* is used when discussing early magnifying instruments, no such name existed in the early 1600s. Galileo called his model an *occhiale* (Italian for "little eye"). The term *microscope* did not become popular until 1625. In a letter written that year describing Galileo's occhiale, scientist Giovanni Faber used "microscope" because it matched "telescope." *Telescope* comes from the Greek words for "to look at something distant," while *microscope* means "to look at something small."

Francesco Stelluti, one of Galileo's followers, used the same term around the same time. Stelluti is the first person known to use a compound microscope for serious scientific studies. In 1625, he observed the bodies of bees and made incredibly detailed drawings. That year, he gave an engraving of those drawings to Pope Urban VIII. Stelluti wanted the pope to see how many wondrous, miniuscule details existed in nature. In the caption for the engraving, he wrote "microscope" to describe the instrument he had used.

The next goal was to produce good lenses faster and more cheaply. To create the clearest image, a lens must be perfectly smooth and symmetrical, with its curves all having the same angles. Doing this by hand was difficult and painfully slow. Italian lens maker Giuseppe Campani solved this problem in 1664 by inventing a tool that could cut perfect spheres of glass. Better glassmaking techniques made a difference, too. Glass containing fewer air bubbles and less dirt produced far crisper images.

The Challenge of Aberration

Next, microscopists looked for ways to deal with ***aberration,*** the distortion or discoloration of a magnified image. One type, called spherical aberration, causes images to be fuzzy around the edges. Dutch astronomer Christiaan Huygens (1629–1695) observed that light rays passing through a convex lens's thick center are slowed down more than those passing through the thin edges. The faster-moving rays focus farther from the lens than do the slower-moving rays. These different focal points cause a fuzzy image. In 1655, Huygens built a new eyepiece that had a convex lens nestled inside a concave lens. These "thickened" edges slowed down the rays and removed the aberration. Robert Hooke liked this design and used it in his microscopes.

A beam of white light passes through a prism and is split into the colors of the spectrum.

Chromatic aberration produces a halo of colored light around an image. As English scientist Sir Isaac Newton (1642–1727) proved in 1666, white light actually contains all the colors of the rainbow. Each color moves through a lens at a different speed and has a slightly different focal point. This effect is exaggerated at the edges of a convex lens. Here light rays are refracted more sharply, causing the colors to appear more clearly. Newton understood how this happened, but he believed there was no solution.

Englishman Chester Moor Hall proved Newton wrong in 1733, when he built a single convex lens using two different types of glass. The light reflecting off a specimen first passed through handmade glass, called crown glass, which split the rays into the colors of the rainbow. The back half of the lens was made from flint glass, which contains lead. The dense lead caused the rainbow colors to bend sharply once again and rejoin into white light. Achromatic, or colorless, lenses similar to these are still used today.

Italian microscope maker Giovanni Battista Amici tried another approach in 1840. He knew that chromatic aberration sometimes occurred because light was refracted around the edges of a lens. To prevent this, he placed a drop of oil on the cover slip over a specimen. When the objective lens came near the cover slip, it was immersed in the oil. As a less-expensive alternative, Amici suggested immersing the lens in water. In the 1870s, fluids were

• Microscopes in the Classroom

Two types of light microscopes are common in modern science classrooms. Dissecting microscopes contain two eyepieces, each with a convex lens. The eyepieces are focused on the same point, creating a three-dimensional image. Dissecting microscopes can achieve magnifications of up to 100X. Specimens are placed on the stage, a flat surface below the lens. The user looks down on the specimen through a pair of viewing tubes. This produces a three-dimensional image, which is focused using a knob. Dissecting microscopes are perfect for examining larger, living specimens.

Many classroom-quality compound microscopes can achieve magnifications up to 1000X, allowing students to see much smaller specimens, but only in two dimensions. A single tube at the top contains the eyepiece lens. Below this is a rotating nosepiece that holds several objective lenses of different strengths. A stage sits a few inches below the nosepiece to hold the specimen. A condenser—usually a mirror or lamp and condensing optics—sits on the base and points toward a hole in the stage. Compound microscopes have a coarse focus knob for making large changes in focus and a fine focus knob for perfecting the focus.

Born in 1786, Giovanni Battista Amici was also a mathematician and astronomer.

discovered that had refraction similar to glass. When lenses were immersed in these fluids, chromatic aberration did not occur. This technique, known as oil immersion, is still used to prevent aberration in high-powered microscopes.

CHAPTER FIVE

Solving Mysteries, Improving Lives

Lenses were invented at a time in European history when books were becoming an important source of knowledge. Magnifying lenses and eyeglasses made it possible for those with weak vision to continue to read as they aged. The popularity of early microscopes inspired people to study nature, as philosophers did during the Roman Empire. And although for a long time microscopes were available only to the wealthy, their popularity

English microscope maker John Marshall based this compound microscope, built about 1710, on Hooke's design.

encouraged lens makers to improve the quality of lenses and seek new ways to use them. The discoveries made by scientists using these improved microscopes would change the world.

Microscopes and Medicine

Medicine was one of the first fields to benefit from microscopes. During the Middle Ages and the Renaissance, Europe was repeatedly swept by waves of illness. Influenza and plague killed millions of people. No logical reason for these epidemics could be identified, and people did not understand how illness and disease can spread throughout a community. Superstition made people believe that illness was a punishment for sin or the result of possession by evil spirits. Leeuwenhoek's discovery of bacteria in 1683 paved the way for other scientists to find a logical and natural explanation for why people got sick.

In the 1850s, the French scientist Louis Pasteur (1822–1895) suggested that microorganisms were the cause of every infectious illness. He developed the theory after being hired by a distiller whose alcohol repeatedly went bad. Pasteur used a microscope to compare normal and spoiled samples of the wine. In both, he saw microscopic organisms that he called germs (Latin for "seed"). Unspoiled samples contained many small, round organisms. When Pasteur heated the wine until these small organisms died, ***fermentation*** stopped. He realized that these must be yeast. Yeast was believed to be a product of fermentation, not the cause of it.

Pasteur used his knowledge of disease-causing organisms to help cure disease in animals and humans.

Pasteur then looked at samples of the spoiled alcohol. He saw many tiny, rod-shaped organisms but fewer yeast. He recognized the rods as bacteria. If he heated the alcohol to just the right temperature, he could kill off the bacteria but keep the yeast alive. After this, the alcohol did not go bad. He concluded that bacteria killed the yeast, which caused the wine to spoil.

The Smallest of the Small

Bacteria are among the smallest organisms able to live independently. The smallest bacterial species discovered so far is *Mycoplasma laidlawii*, which is just 8/1,000,000 of an inch (0.0002 mm) long. At the other end of the spectrum, *Thiomargarita namibiensis* is a bacterium large enough to be seen without a microscope: it measures 0.04 inches (1 mm) across. As a rule, bacteria and other single-celled organisms are small, while organisms with many cells in their bodies tend to grow larger. One exception is the rotifer, a little multicellular animal that lives in freshwater and wet soils. At 16/1,000 of an inch (0.04 mm), rotifers are smaller than many types of bacteria.

After years of research, Pasteur realized that bacteria are responsible for many diseases in humans, animals, and plants, but they are not the cause of all sicknesses. No bacteria could be found in people who suffered colds,

What Is a Virus?

Viruses are so tiny—as much as one hundred times smaller than bacteria—that they cannot be seen through light microscopes. Unlike bacteria, viruses cannot live on their own. Their bodies contain only a bit of genetic material, which they use to reproduce, and are surrounded by a protein "skin." Viruses survive by attaching themselves to living cells inside other organisms. The virus enters a cell, then begins to make copies of itself. Eventually, the new viruses leave the cell and enter new ones, where the replication process begins again. When viruses attack particular organs, such as the lungs or heart, illness results.

influenza, or rabies. Pasteur figured that another, smaller form of life must be responsible. He called these mysterious organisms viruses, using the Latin word for "poisons."

Schleiden and Schwann

When Robert Hooke saw cork cells in the 1660s, he had no idea that they were actually just the "shells" that remain after a plant dies. Microscopists in the mid-nineteenth century explained the role of cells. In 1838, Matthias Schleiden, a German biologist who studied plants, observed a sample of living plant tissue under his microscope. He watched cells reproducing and realized that this is how plants grow. His countryman, Theodor Schwann, made similar observations of many different animals, plants, and microorganisms.

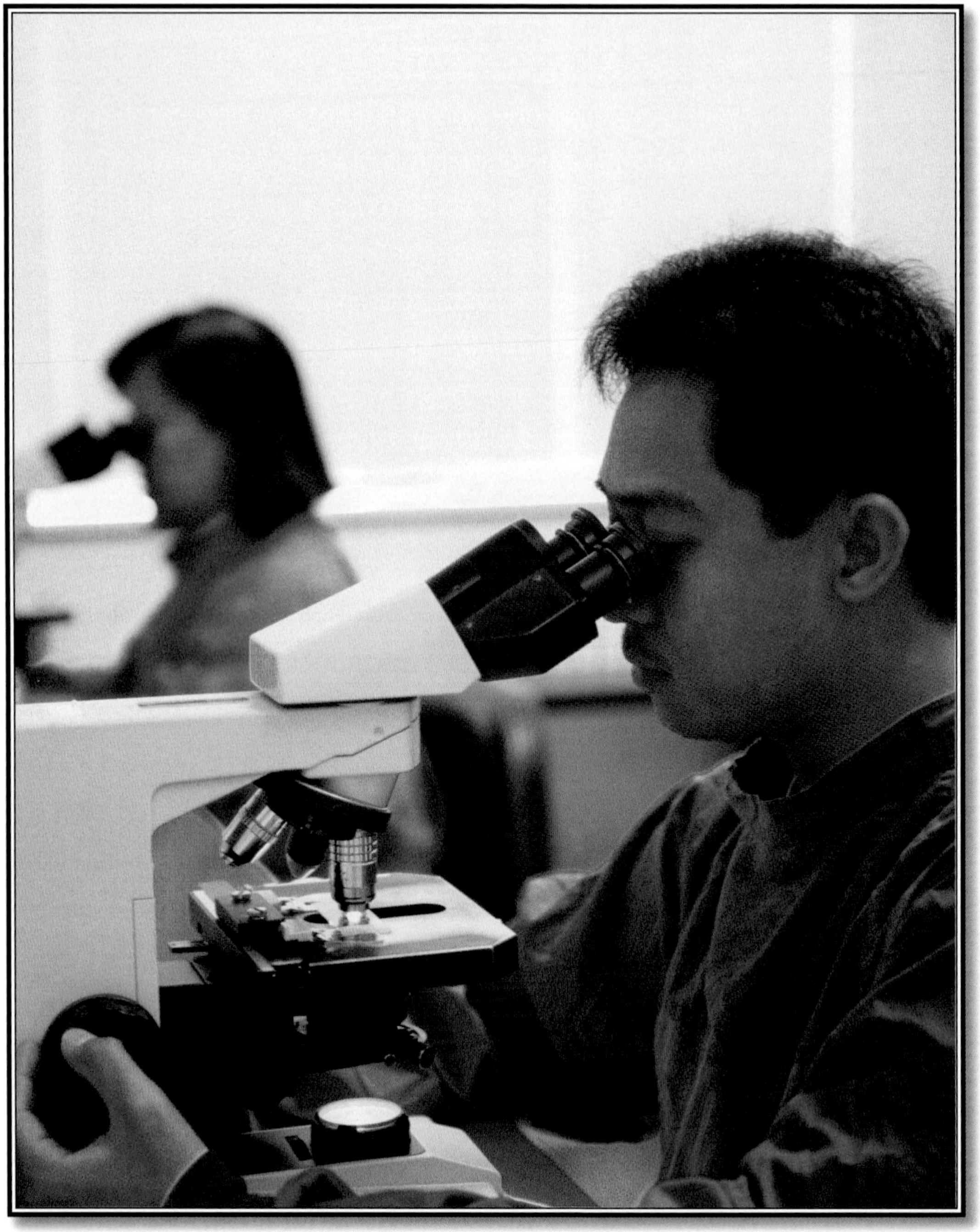

Today, light microscopes are used in classrooms and laboratories throughout the world.

He suggested that all living things are made up of cells. Some forms of life, such as bacteria, consist of only one cell. Others contain millions of cells.

As a result of innovations made over the past three hundred years, light microscopes are widely used throughout modern society. Microscopes help doctors to understand the workings of the human body, to diagnose illness, and to treat injuries. Scientists continue to discover new organisms through microscopes and to gain an increasing understanding of the role microscopic organisms play in the environment. Law enforcement agencies even use microscopes to solve crimes.

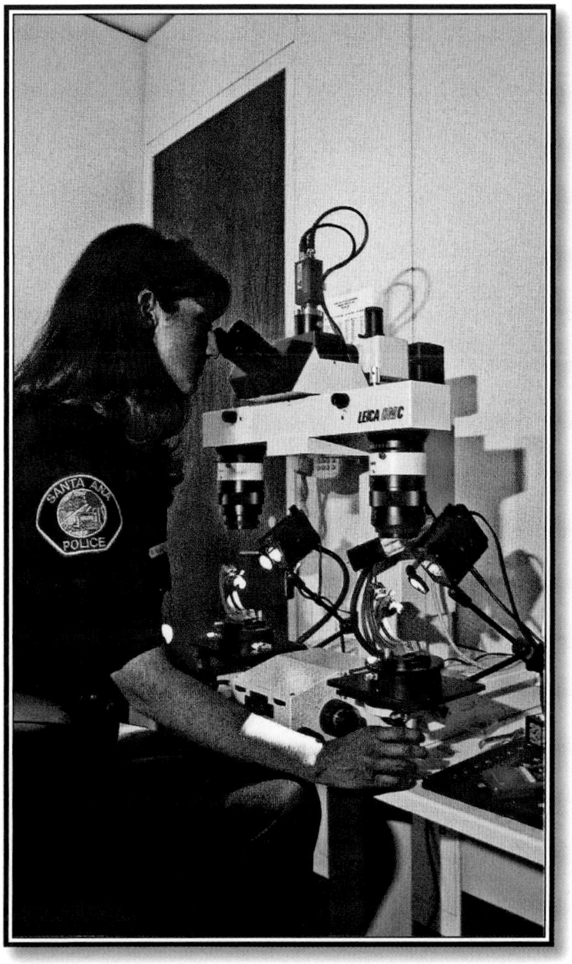

A technician uses a microscope to analyze evidence in a police crime lab in Santa Ana, California.

Advances in Microscopes

In the twentieth century, a whole new group of microscopes was invented. The first of these allowed microscopists to observe the separate parts of cells and bacteria and to identify viruses. By the 1940s, microscopists could see large molecules—including DNA, the molecules inside cells that determine each individual's unique genetic structure. In the 1980s, microscopes became so powerful that they could reveal individual atoms.

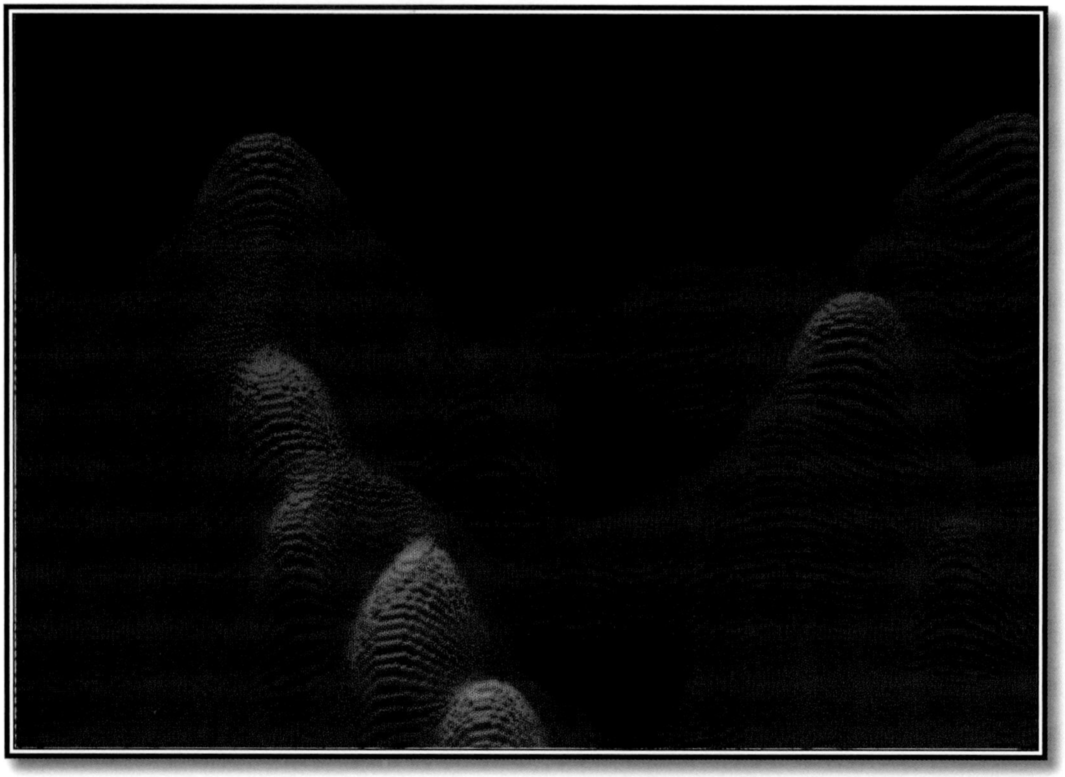

This image of DNA was created using a scanning tunneling microscope (STM). The DNA is shown 2 million times its normal size.

Microscopes are used to manufacture microchips.

These advances have had a profound impact on the world we live in. A better understanding of disease means that people live longer, healthier lives. People's daily lives are more convenient, as well. Microchips, built using powerful microscopes, allow computers the size of books to store many volumes of information and access a global information system, all without the use of wires. Industries also look at the molecular and atomic structure of materials to design amazing products, such as strong but lightweight metals for airplanes, chemicals that create smooth surfaces (such as Teflon), ceramics that protect space shuttles from the burning heat of the atmosphere, and fabrics that resist subzero temperatures. Microscopes have brought monumental changes to society and continue to do so today.

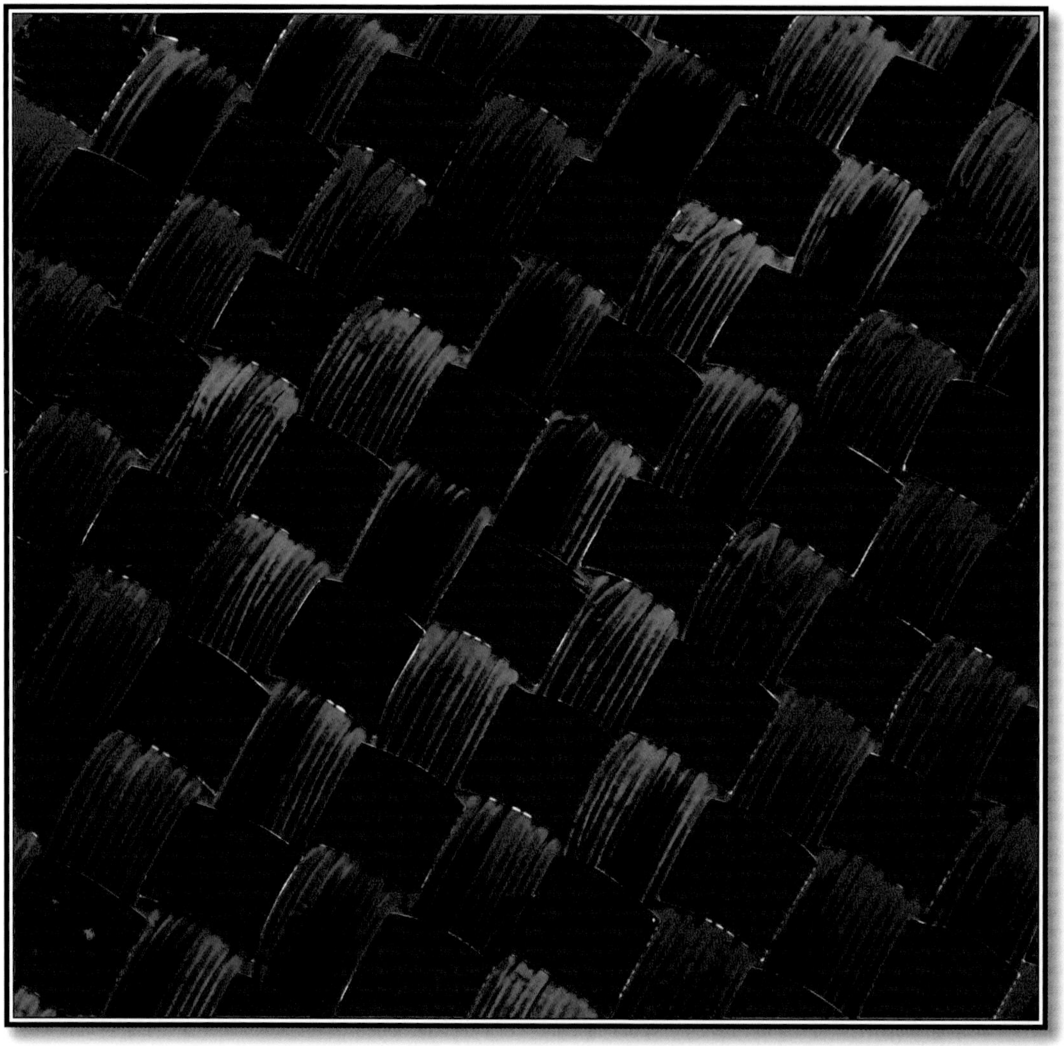

A scanning electron microscope (SEM) was used to create this image of the surface of a waterproof fabric.

CHAPTER SIX

A Small, Small World

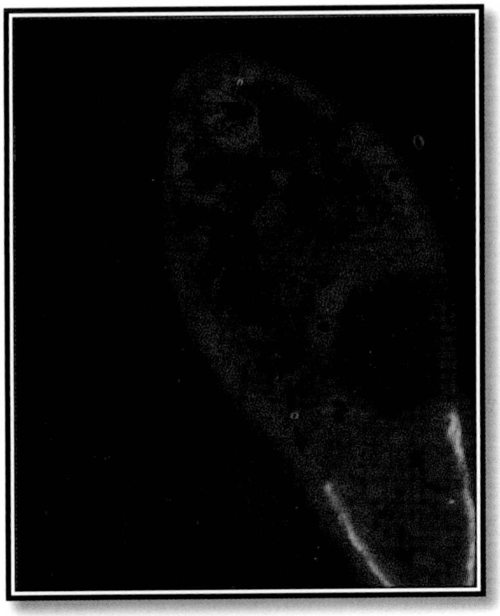

Microscopes allow us to observe single-celled organisms such as this euglena.

Light microscopes allow us to observe parts of the world that are as much as 130 times smaller than the eye can see. Yet scientists faced a problem: even the best light microscope cannot ***resolve,*** or distinguish between, objects that are smaller than half the wavelength of violet light. This means that light microscopes can never produce magnifications greater than

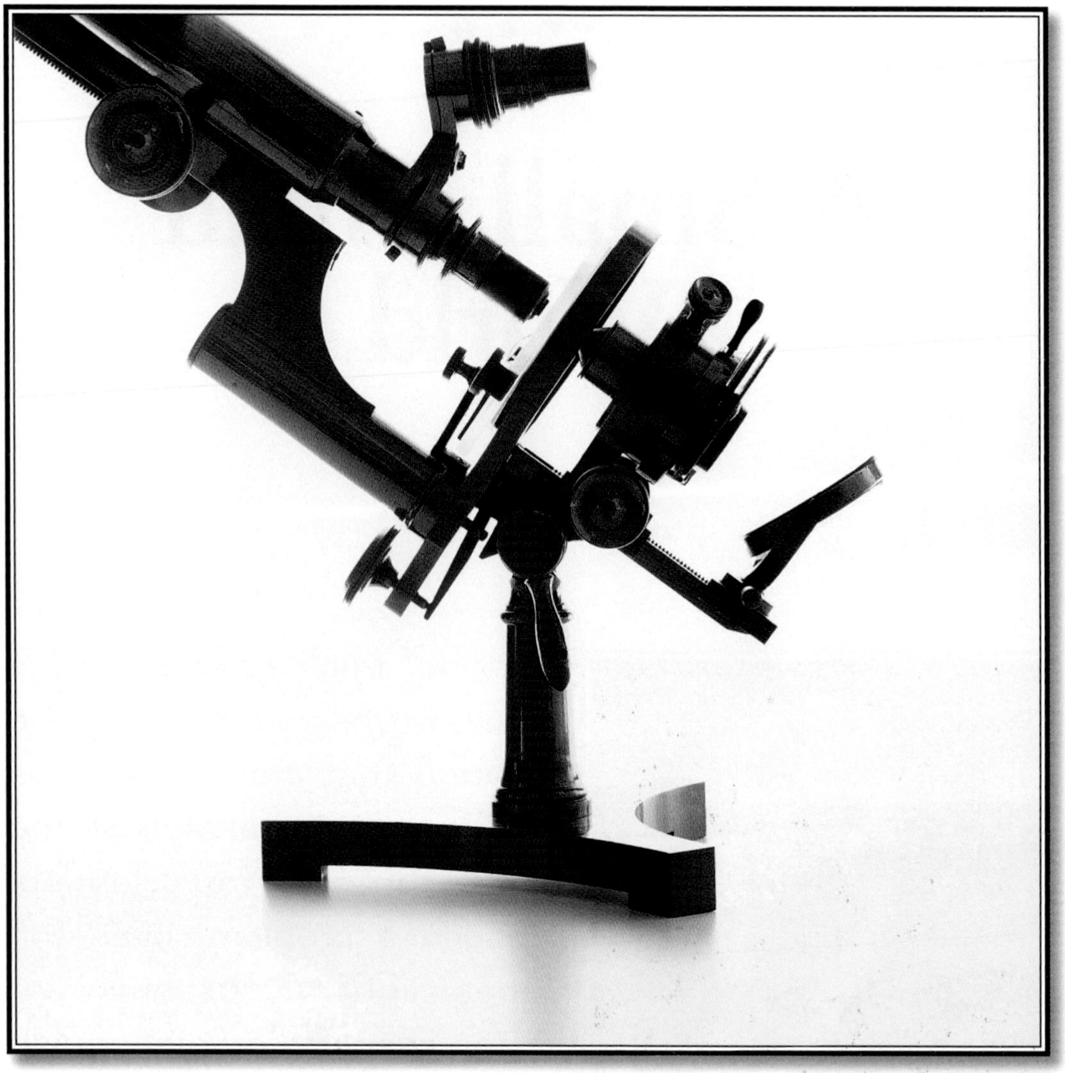

In the nineteenth century, the light microscope was the most advanced tool available for examining microbes.

1,250X. In the late nineteenth century, scientists began to wonder if their exploration of the microscopic world had reached its limits.

Smaller Than an Atom

A breakthrough came with the discovery that light is not the only type of particle that can form waves. Almost 2,500 years ago, the Greek philosopher Democritus suggested that matter is made up of small particles called ***atoms.*** In 1803, a British schoolteacher named John Dalton (1766–1844) proved that every chemical element has a unique type of atom. Almost one hundred years later, British physicist Sir Joseph John Thomson (1856–1940) revealed that atoms are actually made up of even smaller "subatomic" particles. ***Positrons*** are subatomic particles found inside the atom's nucleus. ***Electrons*** float around outside the nucleus. These carry a negative electrical charge, while positrons carry an equal positive charge.

In 1924, French physicist Louis de Broglie (1892–1987) was able to make electrons travel in waves by shooting them through a vacuum—a space without any air. The problem was how to control the direction of the waves.

Sir Joseph John Thomson discovered the electron in 1897. He was awarded the Nobel Prize in Physics in 1906.

An atom is made up of a nucleus, which is a cluster of protons and neutrons that is orbited by a group of electrons. As scientists gained more knowledge of subatomic particles, the stage was set for advances in microscopy.

Dennis Gabor, a Hungarian physicist who lived in the first half of the twentieth century, knew that objects with opposite electrical charges are attracted, while those with similar charges repel each other. When he shot electrons through a negatively charged, doughnut-shaped magnet, they behaved just as he expected: they moved toward the center of the hole. Together, the electrons formed a beam. By rotating the angle of the magnet, the beam could be focused onto a particular spot. Gabor called the magnet an ***electron lens.*** He didn't realize that this technique could be used like a microscope, but another young scientist soon did.

Ernst Ruska received a Nobel Prize in Physics in 1986.

Modern Microscopes

As young Ernst Ruska (1906–1988) pursued his study of electrical engineering in the 1920s, it occurred to him that electron beams might be used for magnification of extremely small objects. Electron wavelengths are about 100,000 times shorter than wavelengths of light. In theory, then, electron waves should be able to reflect

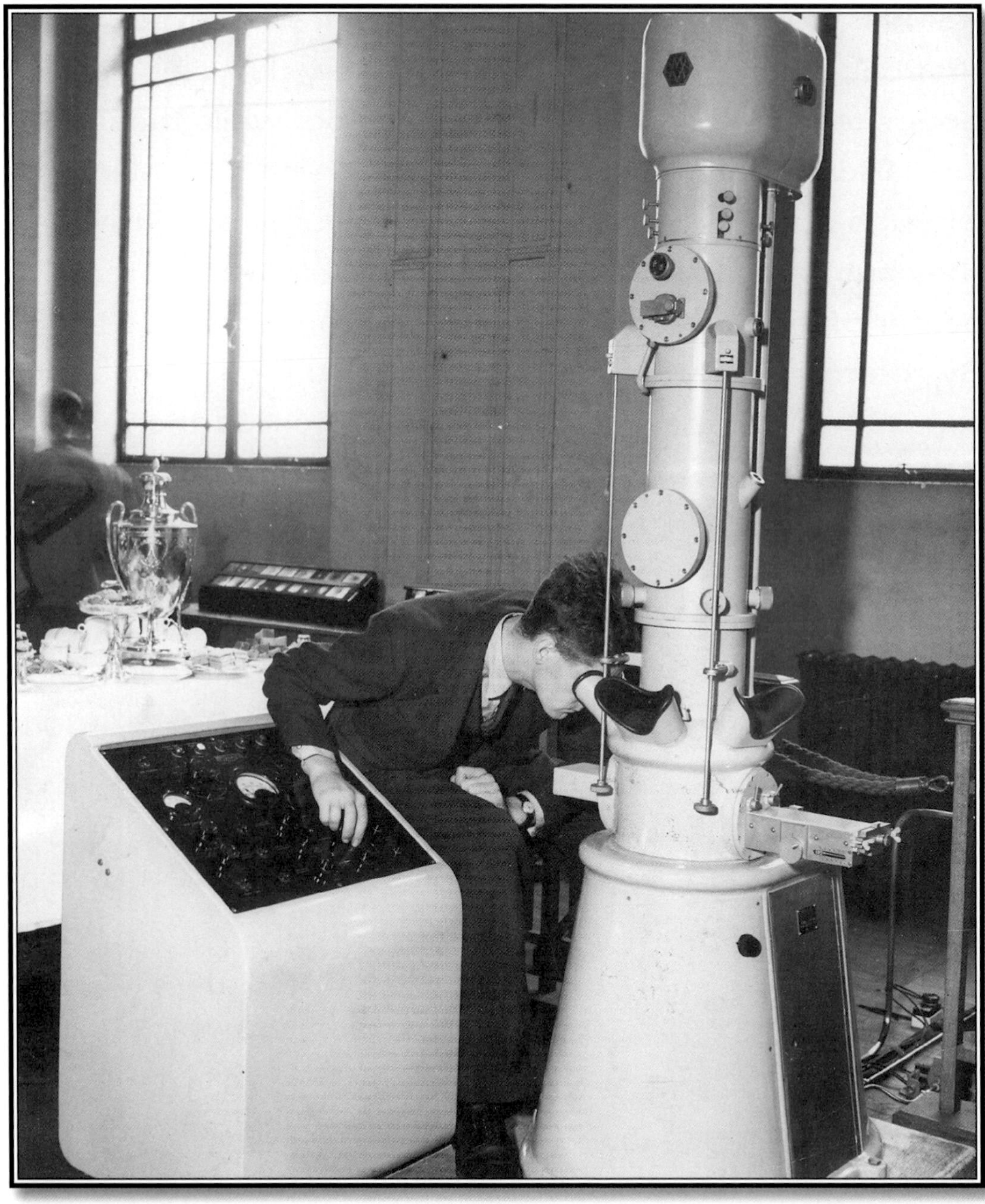

A man learns how an electron microscope works at an exhibit at a science museum in England in 1947.

off objects 100,000 times smaller than light waves can.

In 1931, Ruska and his college professor, Max Knoll, constructed the first ***electron microscope.*** It contained two electron lenses. In the first test, Ruska placed a small piece of cotton in a vacuum-sealed container and bombarded it with a beam of electrons. These went through the cotton, then struck a piece of special photographic paper. Each electron left a mark on the paper. The result was a blurry but identifiable image of the cotton, magnified seventeen times.

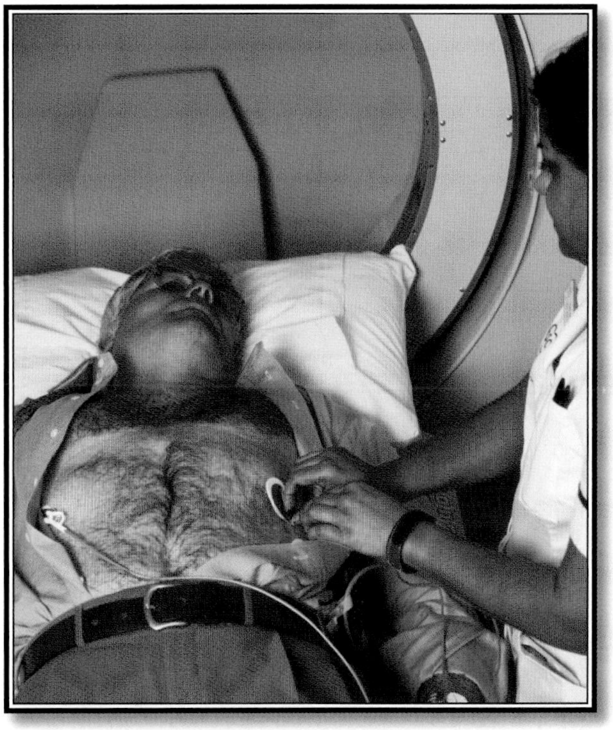

Today, electron beams are used in scanners that create images of internal organs and help doctors diagnose and treat patients.

There were many problems with the microscope, however. The electron current was unsteady, causing the beam to scatter around the viewing chamber rather than flowing in a tidy line. This limited the magnification Ruska could obtain. The beam was incredibly hot, as well, and it

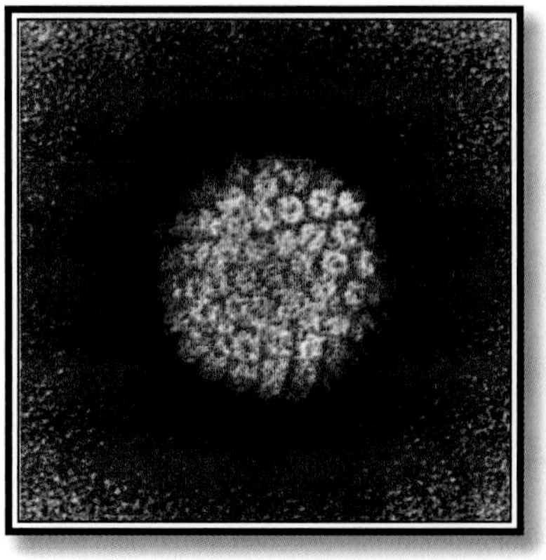

A transmission electron microscope (TEM) image of a virus that causes warts in humans

burned the cotton badly. Another problem with this first model was its sheer size—it stood 8 feet (2.4 meters) tall. It took a few years of work and the efforts of many scientists to make the machine smaller and to narrow the beam for better focus.

The improved instrument, released in 1939, was called a transmission electron microscope (TEM) because a beam of electrons is transmitted, or passed through, the specimen. Ruska's improved TEM produced magnifications up to 500,000X—about 400 times more powerful than the best light microscope.

Ruska Wins the Prize

In 1986, Ernst Ruska was awarded the Nobel Prize in Physics for his invention of the first electron microscope. Upon conferring the prize, the Nobel committee proclaimed that the electron microscope was one of the most important inventions of the twentieth century. Ruska died two years later at the age of eighty-one.

Unlike light waves, electrons cannot pass through a solid object unless it is incredibly thin. For this reason, TEM specimens must be about 1/1,000 the thickness of a sheet of paper. Before viewing, specimens are killed using chemical preparations, then dehydrated. Next, they are treated with resin to keep them from burning. Finally, they are sectioned using glass or diamond knives. A prepared

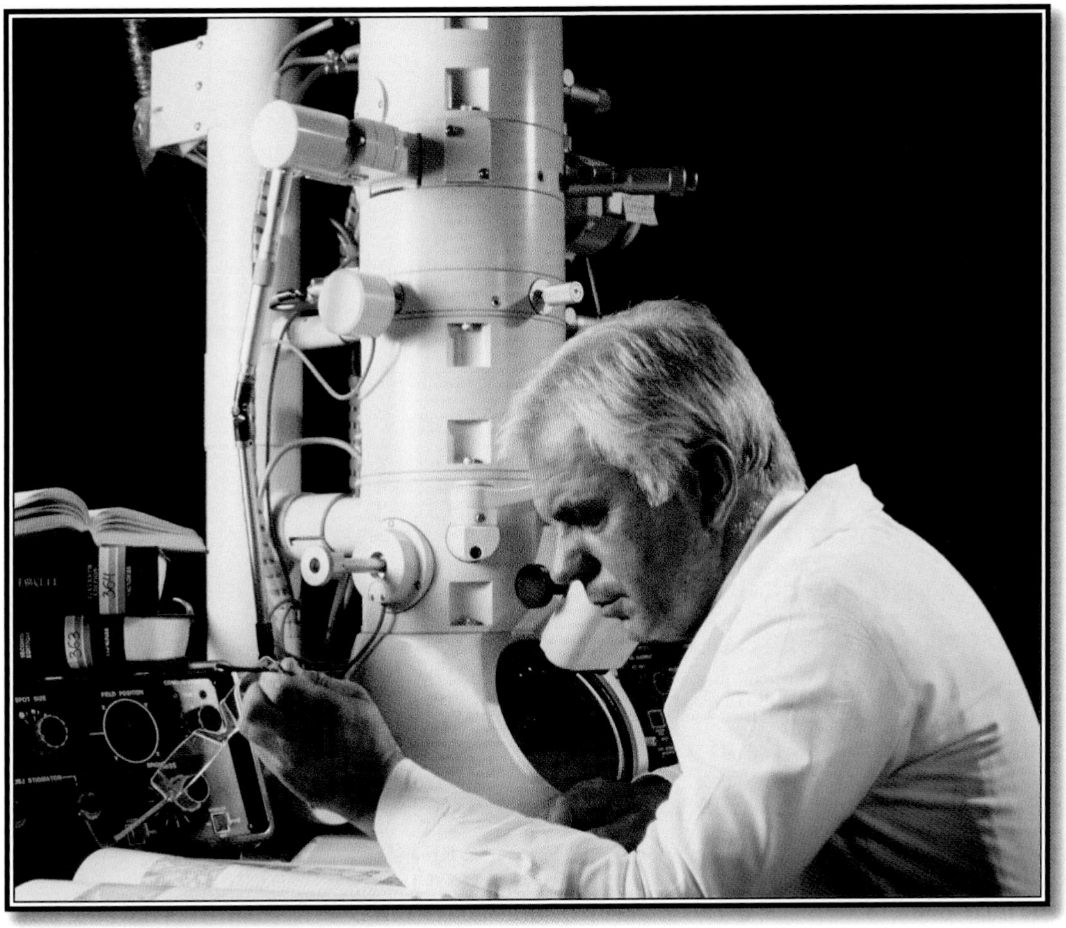

A scientist works with a transmission electron microscope.

A scanning electron microscope (SEM) was used to create this image of a deer tick.

specimen is placed inside a chamber atop a piece of copper wire mesh. Electricity flows through a wire filament at the top of the chamber. As the filament heats up, electrons flow through it. Copper conducts, or carries, electricity, so the electrons are drawn toward the copper mesh on which the specimen rests. Magnetic lenses focus the beam wherever the microscopist wants it to go. The electrons pass through the specimen, then bounce onto a special type of photographic film or onto a digital camera to form a two-dimensional (flat) image.

Scanning electron microscopes (SEM) became available in 1965. They operate by placing a whole specimen (rather than a slice) inside a chamber. After the specimen is treated with a layer of gold or platinum atoms so it will conduct electricity, an electron beam is scanned across its surface. Atoms are knocked away by this impact. These produce an electronic signal, which is converted into an image by a computer. Scanning electron microscopes form a three-dimensional image of the specimen at magnifications up to 300,000X.

The scanning tunneling microscope (STM) was invented by Gerd Binnig and Heinrich Rohrer. In 1986, they were awarded the Nobel Prize in Physics in recognition of their achievement.

Staying Alive

These were great advances, but one problem with electron microscopes can never be resolved. Electrons will move only through a vacuum, which kills living specimens. A group of recently invented microscopes, called ***probe microscopes,*** overcomes this problem. These use microscopically small needles to form images.

The first was the scanning tunneling microscope (STM),

invented in 1981. Its needle skims over a specimen, not touching it but coming incredibly close. The needle senses every change in the object's surface. Electrons from the specimen's surface are attracted to the electrified needle. They jump toward it, creating an electrically charged "tunnel" between the needle and the object. The amount of current detected by the needle is transmitted to a computer, which forms an image. The STM can magnify objects 500,000,000 times—far more than any previous type of microscope. It has given scientists their closest look yet at DNA, viruses, and even individual atoms. Industries use it to manufacture the smallest parts of computers and other incredibly small machines.

The atomic force microscope (AFM) uses a needle made from a splinter of silicon. Researchers at the University of Prince Edward Island in Canada are using the AFM to find out more about how certain vitamins and minerals affect red blood cells. The third, and most recently invented, type of probe is the near-field scanning optical microscope. It uses a tiny laser light to probe the surface of a specimen.

Sound Wave Technology

Another recent innovation in microscopy is the use of sound. ***Acoustic microscopes*** send out sound waves at a frequency far above human hearing. Sound waves do not cause any damage to the specimen; they simply bounce

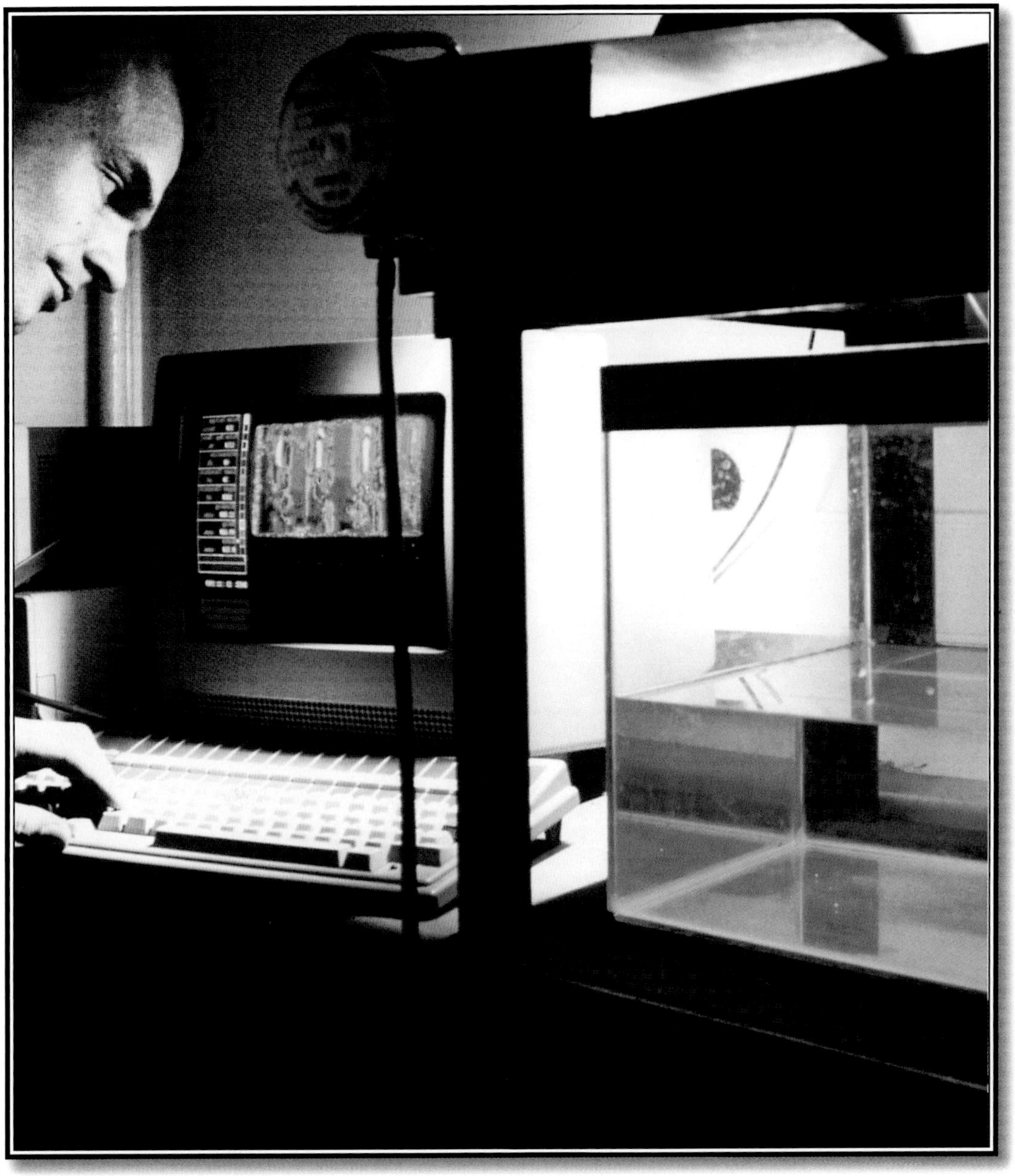

A researcher uses a scanning acoustic microscope to view the structure of a piece of metal. The sample is placed in water because water is a good conductor of sound waves.

A scientist researching diabetes uses a scanning laser acoustic microscope (SLAM) to view cells from a pancreas.

off its surface, forming echoes that are collected by a computer. A map is produced from the echoed sound waves, showing what the specimen looks like. Because sound waves can penetrate matter, they can be focused on any part of the specimen, inside or on its surface. Acoustic microscopy is useful in medical diagnosis, such as finding cancerous growths without exploratory surgery or for examining parts of a complex structure, such as a computer, without disassembling it.

Scanning laser acoustic microscope (SLAM) is a similar technique. The SLAM uses a laser beam to sense how sound waves interact with a specimen. Because sound moves differently through healthy tissue than it does through wounded tissue, SLAM is often used in medicine.

Positron Microscopes

Since 1988, three types of ***positron microscopes*** have been invented. In one, specimens are bombarded with positrons, which pass through them and create an image much like that made by TEM. Scanning positron microscopes (similar to SEM) are often used in electronics manufacturing, telecommunications, and power plants. The third type of positron microscope works in a very different way. Positrons are placed

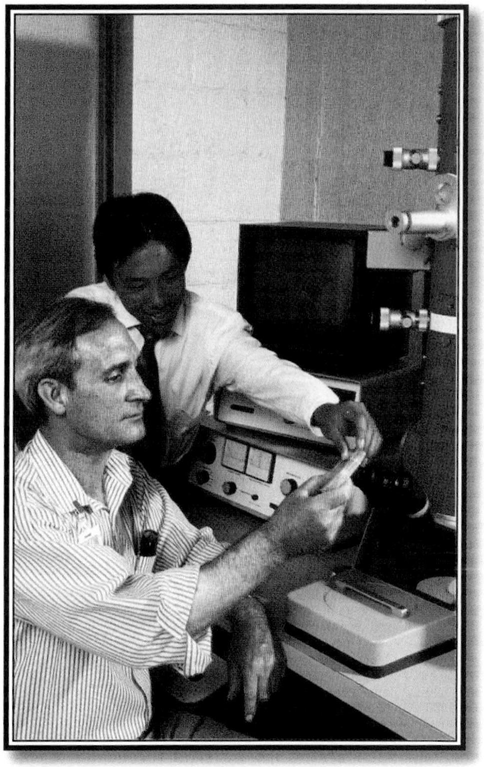

A biologist explains the use of a transmission electron microscope (TEM) to a student.

inside a specimen. As they heat up, they move outward. Parts of the specimen that allow more positrons to escape look different on a computer screen than parts that block the particles' movement.

Microscopic Microscopes

The production of very small microscopes opens up whole new ways of viewing specimens. These miniature machines are called *intravital microscopes*. Connected to video cameras, computers, and monitors, intravital ("inside the body") microscopes can be placed inside patients to find injuries, diagnose diseases, and check the progress of healing down to the cellular level. They also aid surgeons in making fine repairs to blood vessels and nerves after injury.

What Will Be Discovered Next?

In *Micrographia*, Robert Hooke commented on the importance of lenses as tools for discovery. "By the means of Telescopes," he wrote, "there is nothing so far distant but may be represented to our view; and by the help of Microscopes, there is nothing so small as to escape our inquiry." He would be astounded and delighted to learn how much microscopes have revealed about the natural world. Microscopists of the future surely have similar surprises in store.

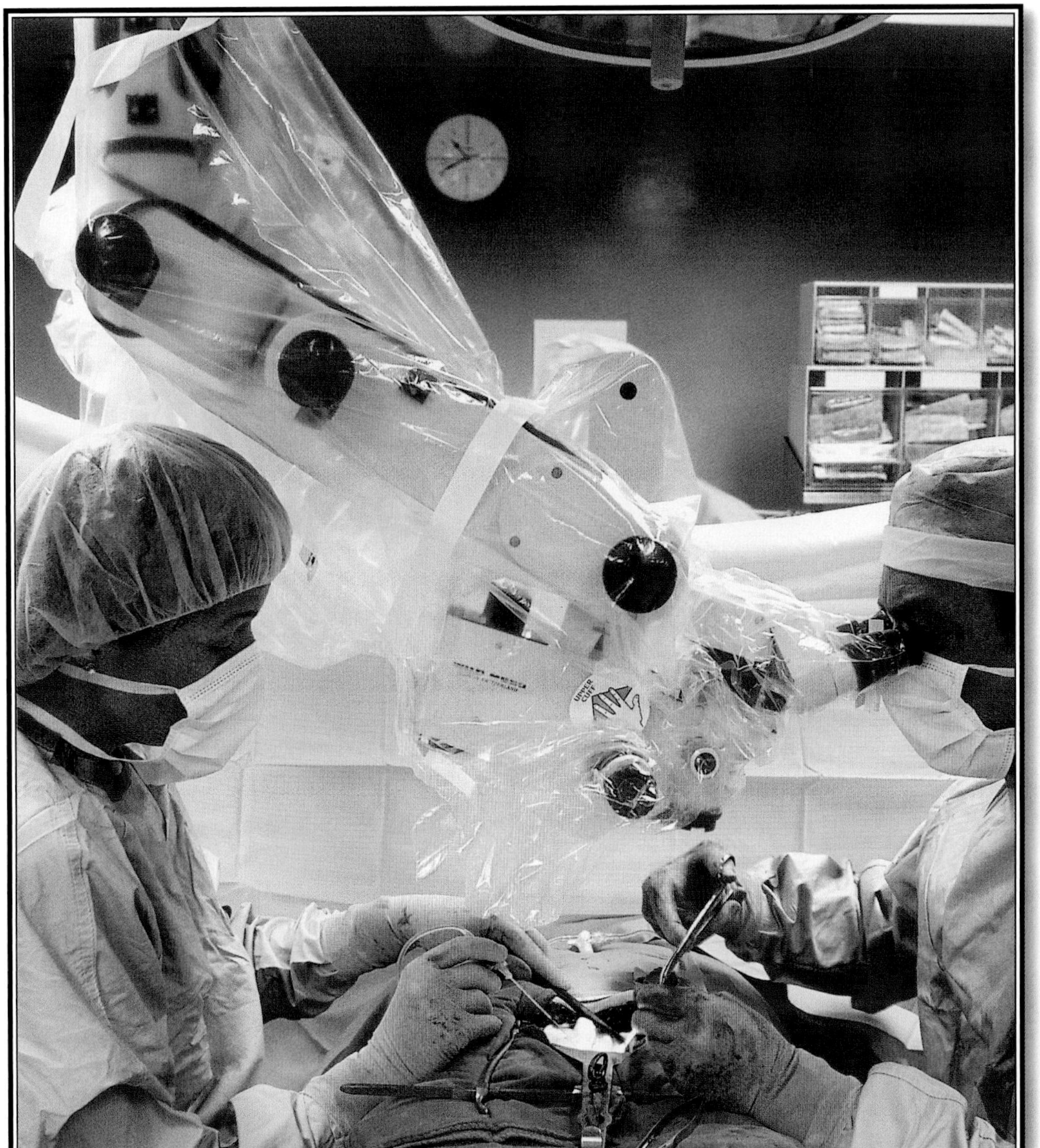

A surgeon performs delicate surgery with the use of a microscope.

The Microscope: A Timeline

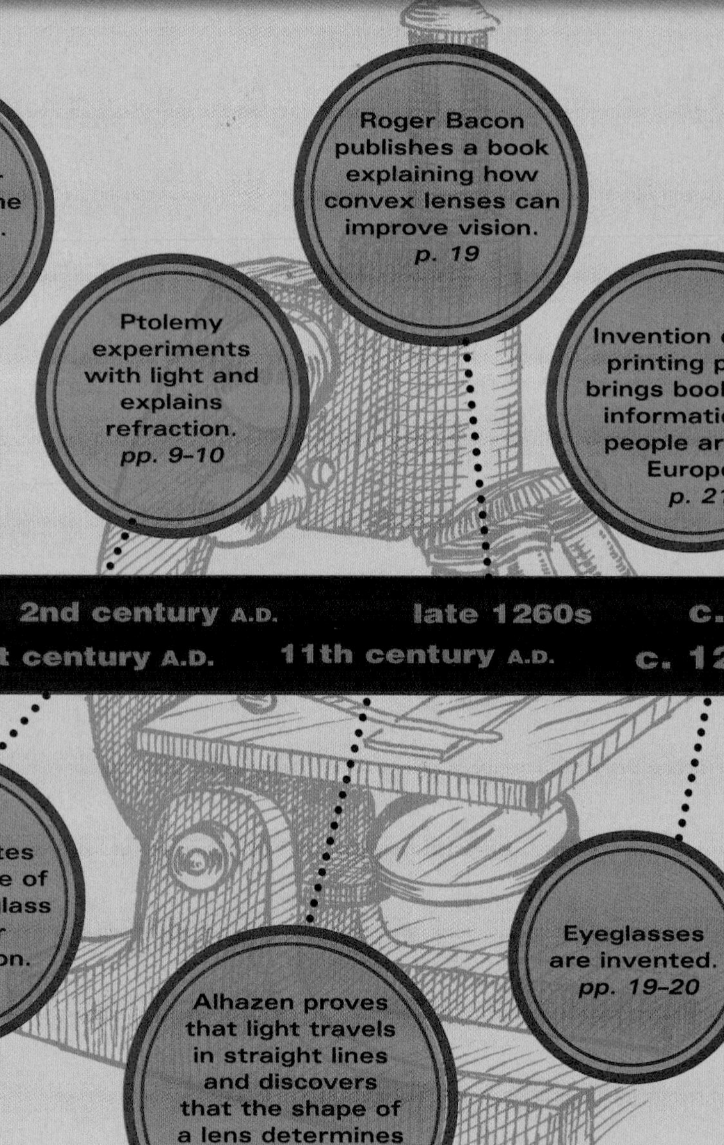

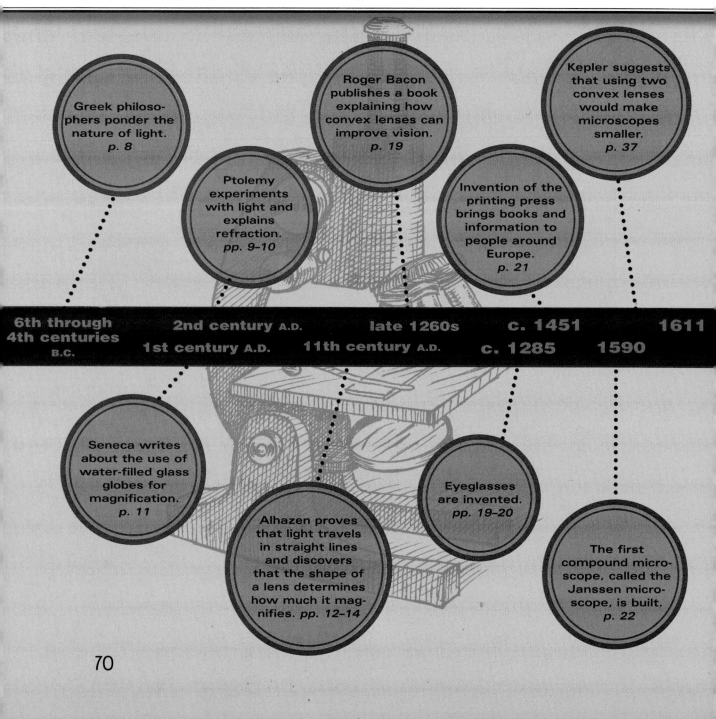

6th through 4th centuries B.C. — Greek philosophers ponder the nature of light. *p. 8*

1st century A.D. — Seneca writes about the use of water-filled glass globes for magnification. *p. 11*

2nd century A.D. — Ptolemy experiments with light and explains refraction. *pp. 9–10*

11th century A.D. — Alhazen proves that light travels in straight lines and discovers that the shape of a lens determines how much it magnifies. *pp. 12–14*

late 1260s — Roger Bacon publishes a book explaining how convex lenses can improve vision. *p. 19*

c. 1285 — Eyeglasses are invented. *pp. 19–20*

c. 1451 — Invention of the printing press brings books and information to people around Europe. *p. 21*

1590 — The first compound microscope, called the Janssen microscope, is built. *p. 22*

1611 — Kepler suggests that using two convex lenses would make microscopes smaller. *p. 37*

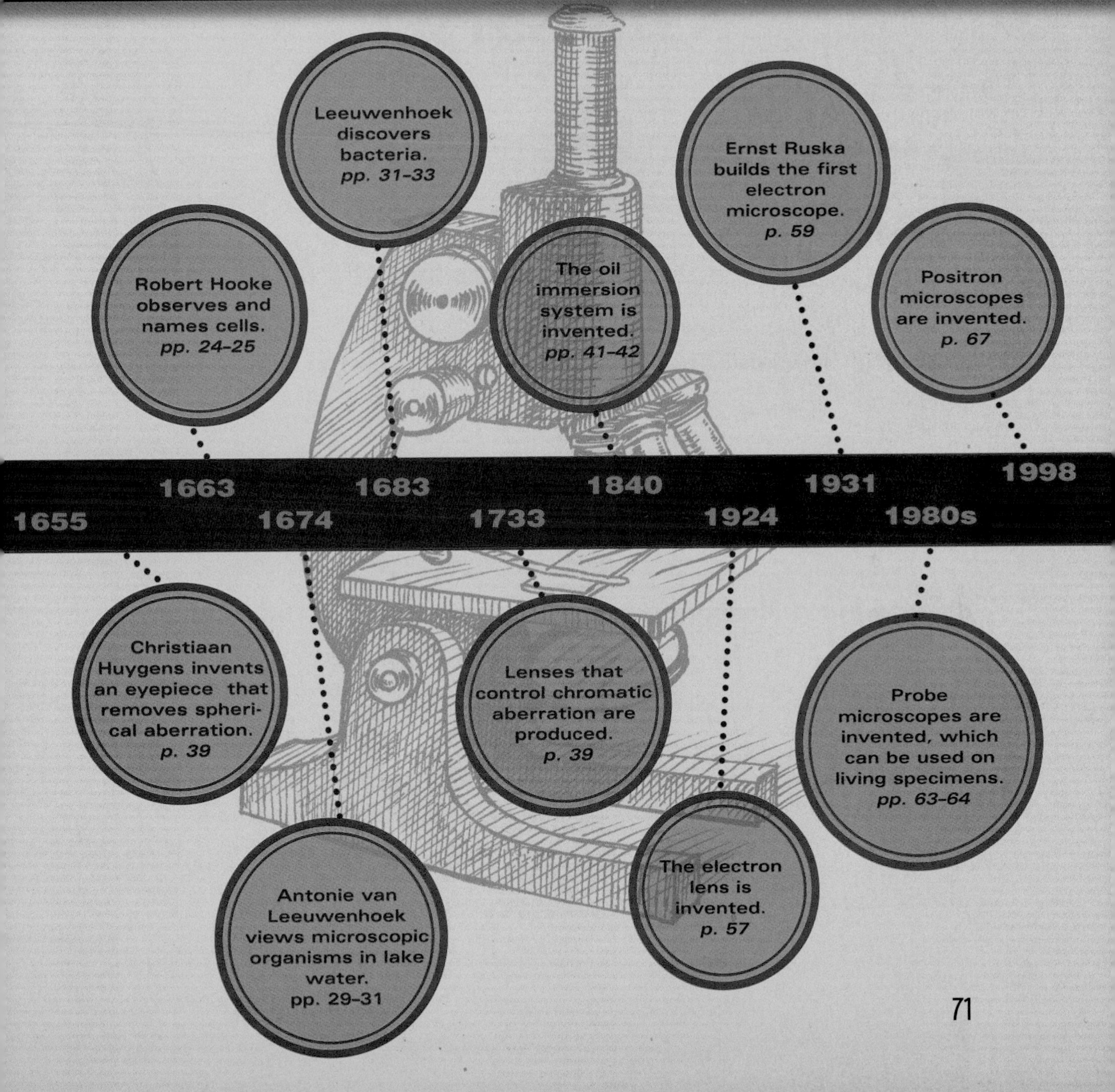
1655
Christiaan Huygens invents an eyepiece that removes spheri-cal aberration. p. 39
1663
Robert Hooke observes and names cells. pp. 24–25
1674
Antonie van Leeuwenhoek views microscopic organisms in lake water. pp. 29–31
1683
Leeuwenhoek discovers bacteria. pp. 31–33
1733
Lenses that control chromatic aberration are produced. p. 39
1840
The oil immersion system is invented. pp. 41–42
1924
The electron lens is invented. p. 57
1931
Ernst Ruska builds the first electron microscope. p. 59
1980s
Probe microscopes are invented, which can be used on living specimens. pp. 63–64
1998
Positron microscopes are invented. p. 67

Glossary

aberration: distortion or discoloration of a magnified image caused by the shape and structure of a lens

acoustic microscope: magnifying instrument that uses sound to form images

atom: the smallest particle of matter that can still be identified as a particular chemical

compound microscope: a magnifying instrument that contains two or more lenses, with one lens magnifying the image of the other lens

concave lens: a lens that is thinner at the center than around the edges

condenser: a mirror that focuses light onto a specimen

convex lens: a lens that is thicker in the center than around the edges

electron: a negatively charged particle found outside the nucleus of atoms

electron lens: a negatively charged magnet used to focus a beam of electrons onto a specimen

electron microscope: a magnifying instrument that uses negatively charged atomic particles to form images

fermentation: a chemical change that occurs when enzymes break down organic compounds

focal length: the distance between a lens and the point where light rays focus after passing through it

intravital microscope: a very small magnifying instrument that can be placed inside the body of a patient

lens: a curved piece of glass or other clear material that is used to bend (refract) light or other waves

magnify: to make an object appear larger

media: substances that reflect light differently

optics: the study of light

positron: a positively charged particle, with the same mass as an electron, found inside the nucleus of atoms; when brought together, positrons and electrons will destroy each other

positron microscope: a magnifying instrument that uses positively charged electrons to form images

probe microscope: a magnifying instrument with needles that hover near the surface of objects to form images

reflect: to bounce off

refraction: the bending of light rays when they pass from one medium to another

resolve: to be able to distinguish between two closely spaced objects

simple microscope: a magnifying instrument that contains one lens

To Find Out More

Books

Goldstein, D. J. *Understanding the Light Microscope: A Computer-Aided Instruction.* Burlington, Mass.: Academic Press, 1999.

Kramer, Stephen P. *Hidden Worlds: Looking Through a Scientist's Microscope.* Boston: Houghton Mifflin, 2001.

Rogers, Kirsteen, and Paul Dowswell (ed.). *The Usborne Internet-Linked Complete Book of the Microscope.* London: Usborne Books, 2002.

Snedden, Robert. *Scientists, Discoveries, and Inventions.* Chicago: Heinemann Library, 2000.

Stewart, Gail B. *Microscopes.* San Diego: Lucent Books, 2003.

Multimedia Resource

"How to Use a Microscope." (DVD) Educational Video Network, Inc., 2004.

Web Sites

How Light Works

http://www.science.howstuffworks.com/light.htm

For information on light, including reflection, absorption, scattering, refraction, and more.

Microbe Zoo

http://commtechlab.msu.edu/sites/dlc-me/zoo/

Click on a site in the microbe zoo and discover the microbes that exist there. You don't even need a microscope!

Optics for Kids

http://www.opticsforkids.com/index.cfm

Here you'll find fun facts about optics, as well as games, experiments, and much more.

Organization

The Microscopy Society of America

230 East Ohio Street, Suite 400

Chicago, IL 60611

This society exists to promote and communicate advances in microscopy. It is open to student membership.

Index

About the Author

As a science teacher, Christine Petersen often uses microscopes with her students. Before writing this book, however, she didn't know much about the history of their invention. The library at her school turned out to be a great resource. In it, she found books about scientists and their discoveries, and was able to get specific information about the physics of light and magnification. She also accessed online databases from her community library's Web site.

When she's not writing or teaching, Ms. Petersen spends time with her young son and enjoys snowshoeing, canoeing, and bird-watching. She has written more than a dozen previous books, including *Rosie the Riveter*, *The Iran-Contra Scandal*, *Water Power*, and *Land Conservation*.